...per is a successful man. ... ...nable, interesting, amusing, and clever.

His daughter Catherine is none of those things. She is a good, simple girl, who loves and admires her father and always tries hard to please him, but she is a great disappointment to him. Dr Sloper does not expect any interest or excitement from Catherine.

But life in Washington Square does become rather exciting, after all. Romance arrives, in the shape of a handsome young man who comes to court Catherine. This pleases Catherine's foolish aunt, Mrs Penniman, very much; she thinks Morris Townsend is charming, and so of course does Catherine. Dr Sloper, however, looks at young Mr Townsend rather differently. The Doctor is a rich man, and is conscious that after his death Catherine will inherit a fortune of 30,000 dollars a year. He wonders why such a charming and handsome young man is courting his dull daughter . . .

OXFORD BOOKWORMS LIBRARY
Classics

Washington Square

Stage 4 (1400 headwords)

Series Editor: Jennifer Bassett
Founder Editor: Tricia Hedge
Activities Editors: Jennifer Bassett and Alison Baxter

HENRY JAMES

Washington Square

Retold by
Kieran McGovern

OXFORD UNIVERSITY PRESS

Oxford University Press
Great Clarendon Street, Oxford OX2 6DP

Oxford New York
Athens Auckland Bangkok Bogotá Buenos Aires Cape Town
Chennai Dar es Salaam Delhi Florence Hong Kong Istanbul Karachi Kolkata
Kuala Lumpur Madrid Melbourne Mexico City Mumbai Nairobi
Paris São Paulo Shanghai Singapore Taipei Tokyo Toronto Warsaw
with associated companies in
Berlin Ibadan

OXFORD and OXFORD ENGLISH
are trade marks of Oxford University Press

ISBN 0 19 423052 X

This simplified edition © Oxford University Press 2000

Third impression 2001

First published in Oxford Bookworms 1998
This second edition published in the Oxford Bookworms Library 2000

A complete recording (in American English) of this Bookworms edition of
Washington Square is available on cassette ISBN 0 19 423150 X

Illustrated by John Holder

Printed in Spain by Unigraf s.l.

CONTENTS

1
Poor Catherine

In the first half of the nineteenth century there lived in New York a very successful doctor. His success was for two reasons. He was, without doubt, a good doctor, intelligent and honest, but he also knew how to please his patients. He gave long, careful explanations about the illness, and always gave them some medicine to take. Indeed, his patients were fond of saying that they had the best doctor in the country.

By the time he was fifty, Doctor Austin Sloper was quite a famous person in New York. His conversation was clever and amusing, and no fashionable party in the city was complete without him.

He was also lucky. In 1820, at the age of twenty-seven, he had married, for love, a very charming girl, who had a fortune of ten thousand dollars a year. For about five years Doctor Sloper was a very happy husband; he continued to work as a doctor and each year became more experienced and more successful.

Some of the experience, however, was very unwelcome. His first child, a little boy of great promise, died at three years of age. Neither the mother's love nor the father's medicine could save him. Two years later Mrs Sloper had a second child, a little girl. This disappointed the Doctor, who had wished for another son to take the place of the first, but there was worse news to come. A week after the child was born, the young mother fell ill, and before another week had passed, she was dead.

For a man whose profession was to keep people alive, Austin Sloper had certainly done badly in his own family, but the only person who blamed Doctor Sloper was Doctor Sloper himself. He felt that he had failed, and he carried this private blame for the rest of his life.

He still had his little girl, whom he named Catherine after her poor mother. She grew up a strong and healthy child, and her father knew that he would not lose her.

When the child was about ten years old, the Doctor invited his sister, Mrs Lavinia Penniman, to stay with him. He had two sisters and both of them had married early in life. The younger one, Mrs Almond, was the wife of a rich man and the mother of a large family. Elizabeth Almond was a comfortable, reasonable woman and Doctor Sloper preferred her to his sister Lavinia. However, Lavinia's husband had died at the age of thirty-three, leaving his wife without children or fortune, and so Doctor Sloper invited his sister to stay while she looked for rooms to rent. No one really knew if Mrs Penniman ever looked for rooms, but it is certain that she never found them.

After six months the Doctor accepted the fact that his sister was never going to leave. Mrs Penniman told everyone except her brother that she was Catherine's teacher. Doctor Sloper guessed that this was her explanation, and he found the idea laughable since he did not think his sister was very intelligent. In fact, he did not have a good opinion of women at all. The only woman he had ever admired had been his wife.

He was always extremely polite to Lavinia, but he had no interest in her opinions or conversation. He only spoke to her to inform her of his wishes for Catherine.

Once, when the girl was about twelve years old, he said to his sister, 'Try to make a clever woman out of her, Lavinia. I should like her to be a clever woman.'

Mrs Penniman looked at him. 'My dear Austin,' she said, 'do you think it is better to be clever than to be good?'

'Good for what?' asked the Doctor. 'You are good for nothing unless you are clever. Of course I wish Catherine to be good, but it will not make her a better person to be a fool.'

Mrs Penniman was a tall, thin, fair woman. She was romantic, and her brother knew that she loved little secrets and mysteries.

'When Catherine is about seventeen,' he said to himself, 'Lavinia will try and persuade her that some young man with a moustache is in love with her. It will be quite untrue. No young man, with or without a moustache, will ever be in love with Catherine.'

Catherine was strong and healthy, but she did not have any of her mother's beauty or her father's cleverness – in fact, there was very little that was interesting about her at all. She was large and well built, with brown hair, a round face, and small, quiet eyes. The more generous friends of Doctor Sloper noticed that she was well behaved and polite; others thought she was just dull. But Catherine was not someone people spent much time talking about.

She was extremely fond of her father and very much afraid of him. She wanted to please him more than anything in the world, but although Doctor Sloper was usually kind to Catherine, he was very disappointed in her. He wanted to be proud of his daughter, but there was nothing to be proud of in poor Catherine. She was not elegant or pretty or charming like her mother. And by the age of eighteen Mrs Penniman had still not made her a clever woman.

Over the years, however, Doctor Sloper got used to his disappointment. 'I expect nothing from her,' he said to himself. 'If she gives me a surprise, I will be happy. If she doesn't, I shall not lose anything.'

At this time it did not seem possible that Catherine would ever surprise anyone. She was always very quiet, saying so little in conversation that she seemed almost stupid. But she was silent because she was shy, uncomfortably, painfully shy. In fact, she was a very gentle, sensitive girl.

Slowly Catherine realized that she was changing from a girl into a young lady. She began wearing expensive clothes in very bright colours – rather too bright for Doctor Sloper. When she was twenty, she bought a red and gold evening dress, and did not seem to realize that it made her look ten years older. Doctor Sloper preferred simple, elegant things, and it annoyed him to think that his child was both ugly and badly dressed, though he kept this opinion private.

It must be added that Catherine was expected to become a very rich woman. She had already inherited some money from her mother, but the Doctor had been making twenty thousand dollars a year by his profession and saving half of it. One day, this growing fortune would pass to Catherine.

In 1835 Doctor Sloper moved his family to a more fashionable address. He built himself a handsome, modern

Catherine was always very quiet, saying so little in conversation that she seemed almost stupid.

house in Washington Square, which was just around the corner from Fifth Avenue. Across the road from the house, in the centre of the square, was a pretty garden, which was open to everyone though few people ever used it.

Mrs Almond lived further out of the city in a house that was almost in the country. She had nine children, and Catherine went with Mrs Penniman to see her cousins every week. The little Almonds were now growing up; the boys had been sent off to college or to work in offices, while the girls looked for suitable husbands.

When Mrs Almond gave a party for her younger daughter Marian, who had become engaged to a promising young man, Catherine, naturally, was invited. At this time she was twenty-one years old, and Mrs Almond's party was the beginning of something very important.

2
A handsome young man

Not long after the dancing had begun at the party, Marian Almond came up to introduce Catherine to a tall young man. She told Catherine that the young man very much wanted to meet her, and that he was a cousin of Arthur Townsend, the man she was engaged to.

Catherine always felt uncomfortable when meeting new people. The young man, Mr Morris Townsend, was very handsome, and when Marian went away, Catherine stood in front of him, not knowing what to say. But before she could get embarrassed, Mr Townsend began to talk to her with an easy smile.

'What a delightful party! What a charming house! What an interesting family! What a pretty girl your cousin is!'

Mr Townsend looked straight into Catherine's eyes. She answered nothing; she only listened, and looked at him. He went on to say many other things in the same comfortable and natural way. Catherine, though silent, was not embarrassed; it seemed right that such a handsome man should talk, and that she should simply look at him.

The music, which had been silent for a while, suddenly began again. He smiled and asked her to dance. Catherine gave no answer, she simply let him put his arm around her, and in a moment they were dancing around the room. When they paused, she felt that she was red, and then, for some moments, she stopped looking at him.

'Does dancing make you dizzy?' he asked, in a kind voice.

Catherine looked up at him. 'Yes,' she murmured, though she did not know why; dancing had never made her dizzy.

'Then we will sit and talk,' said Mr Townsend. 'I will find a good place to sit.'

He found a good place – a charming place; a little sofa in a corner that seemed meant for two persons.

'*We* will talk,' the young man had said; but he still did all the talking. Catherine sat with her eyes fixed on him, smiling, and thinking him very clever. She had never seen anyone so handsome before.

He told her that he was a distant cousin of Arthur Townsend, and Arthur had brought him to introduce him to the family. In fact, he was a stranger in New York – he had not been there for many years. He had been travelling around the world, living in many strange places, and had only come back a month or two before. New York was very pleasant, but he felt lonely.

'People forget you,' he said, smiling at Catherine.

It seemed to Catherine that no one who had seen him would ever forget him, but she kept this thought to herself.

They sat there for some time. He was very amusing, and Catherine had never heard anyone speak as well as he did – not even an actor in a theatre. And Mr Townsend was not like an actor; he seemed so sincere, so natural.

Then Marian Almond came pushing through the crowd of dancers. She gave a little cry, which made Catherine blush, when she saw the young people still together. She told Mr Townsend that her mother had been waiting for half an hour to introduce him to somebody.

'We shall meet again,' he said to Catherine, as he left her.

Her cousin took Catherine by the arm. 'And what do you think of Morris?' she asked.

'Oh, nothing particular,' Catherine answered, hiding what she really felt for the first time in her life.

'Oh, I must tell him that!' cried Marian. 'It will do him good. He's so terribly conceited.'

'Conceited?' said Catherine, staring at her cousin.

'So Arthur says, and Arthur knows about him.'

'We shall meet again,' Mr Townsend said to Catherine.

'Oh, don't tell him!' said Catherine.

'Don't tell him! I have told him that many times.'

Half an hour later Catherine saw her Aunt Penniman sitting by a window, with Morris Townsend – she already knew the name very well – standing in front of her. He was saying clever things, and Mrs Penniman was smiling.

Catherine moved away quickly; she did not want him to

turn round and see her. But she was glad he was talking to Mrs Penniman because it seemed to keep him near to her.

In the carriage, as they drove home, Catherine was very quiet, and Doctor Sloper talked with his sister.

'Who was that young man you spent so much time with?' he asked. 'He seemed very interested in you.'

'He was not interested in me,' said Mrs Penniman. 'He talked to me about Catherine.'

'Oh, Aunt Penniman!' Catherine murmured.

'He is very handsome and very clever,' her aunt went on. 'He spoke in a – in a very charming way.'

The Doctor smiled. 'He is in love with Catherine, then?'

'Oh, father!' murmured the girl, thankful that it was dark in the carriage.

'I don't know that; but he admired her dress.'

Admiring just the dress, instead of the person, might not seem very enthusiastic, but Catherine did not think this. She was deeply pleased.

Her father looked, with a cool little smile, at her expensive red and gold dress. 'You see,' he said, 'he thinks you have eighty thousand dollars a year.'

'I don't believe he thinks of that,' said Mrs Penniman; 'he is too fine a gentleman.'

'He must be extremely fine not to think of that!'

'Well, he is!' Catherine cried, before she knew it.

'I thought you had gone to sleep,' her father answered. 'The hour has come!' he added to himself. 'Lavinia is going to arrange a romance for Catherine.'

A few days after Mrs Almond's party, Morris Townsend and his cousin called at Washington Square. Catherine and her aunt were sitting together by the fire in the parlour.

Arthur Townsend sat and talked to Catherine, while his companion sat next to Mrs Penniman. Catherine, usually so easy to please, tonight found Arthur rather uninteresting. She kept looking over at the other side of the room, where Morris Townsend was deep in conversation with her aunt. Every few minutes he looked over at Catherine and smiled, and she wished that she was sitting nearer to him.

Arthur seemed to notice that Catherine was interested in his companion. 'My cousin asked me to bring him,' he explained. 'He seemed to want very much to come. I told him I wanted to ask you first, but he said that Mrs Penniman had invited him.'

'We are very glad to see him,' said Catherine. She wished to talk more about him, but she did not know what to say. 'I never saw him before,' she went on.

Arthur Townsend stared. 'But he told me he talked with you for over half an hour the other night.'

'I mean before the other night. That was the first time.'

'Oh, he has been away from New York – he has been all round the world.'

'My aunt likes him very much,' said Catherine.

'Most people like him – he's so brilliant – though I know some people who say my cousin is too clever.'

Catherine listened with extreme interest. If Morris Townsend had a fault, it would naturally be that one, she

11

thought. After a moment she asked, 'Now that he has come back, will he stay here always?'

'If he can find something to do,' said Arthur. 'He's looking around for some kind of employment or business, but he can't find anything.'

'I am very sorry,' said Catherine.

'Oh, he doesn't mind,' Arthur said. 'He isn't in a hurry.'

Catherine thought about this, then asked, 'Won't his father take him into his business – his office?'

'He hasn't got a father – he has only got a sister,' said Arthur Townsend. And he looked across at his cousin and began to laugh. 'Morris, we're talking about you.'

Morris Townsend paused in his conversation with Mrs Penniman, and stared, with a little smile. Then he stood up.

'I'm afraid I was not talking about you,' he said to Catherine's companion. 'Though I can't pretend that Miss Sloper's name did not enter our conversation.'

Catherine thought that this was a wonderfully clever thing to say, but she was embarrassed by it, and she also got up. Morris Townsend stood looking at her and smiling; he put out his hand to say goodbye. He was going, and though he had not said anything to Catherine, she was still glad that she had seen him.

'I will tell her what you have said – when you go!' said Mrs Penniman with a little laugh.

Catherine blushed – she felt they were almost laughing at her. What in the world had this beautiful young man said? She saw that he was looking at her kindly.

12

*Every few minutes Morris Townsend looked over
at Catherine and smiled.*

'I have not talked with you,' he said, 'and that was what I
came for. But it will be a good reason for coming another time.
I am not afraid of what your aunt will say when I go.'

After the two young men had left, Catherine, who was still
blushing, gave Mrs Penniman a serious look.

'What did you say you would tell me?' she asked.

Mrs Penniman smiled and nodded a little. 'It's a great

secret, my dear child, but he is coming here to court you!'

Catherine was serious still. 'Is that what he told you?'

'He didn't say so exactly, but he left me to guess it. I'm good at guessing.' Mrs Penniman gave her niece a soft little kiss. 'You must be very nice to him.'

Catherine stared – she was amazed. 'I don't understand you,' she said. 'He doesn't know me.'

'Oh yes, he does. He knows you more than you think. I have told him all about you.'

'Oh, Aunt Penniman!' said Catherine in a frightened voice. 'He is a stranger – we don't know him.'

'My dear Catherine, you know very well that you admire him.'

'Oh, Aunt Penniman!' said Catherine again. Perhaps she did admire him – though this did not seem to her a thing to talk about. But she could not believe that this brilliant stranger wished to court her; only a romantic woman like her aunt would believe that.

3
Who is Morris Townsend?

Half an hour after the two young men had left, Doctor Sloper came into the parlour.

'Mr Morris Townsend has just been here, Austin,' Mrs Penniman told her brother. 'What a pity you missed him.'

'Who in the world is Mr Morris Townsend?'

'The gentleman at Elizabeth's party who liked Catherine so much,' said Mrs Penniman.

'Oh, his name is Morris Townsend, is it?' the Doctor said. He looked at Catherine. 'And did he come here to ask you to marry him?'

'Oh, father!' murmured Catherine, turning away.

'I hope he won't do that without your permission,' said Mrs Penniman.

'My dear, he seems to have yours,' her brother answered. 'The next time he comes, you should call me. He might like to see me.'

Morris Townsend came again five days later, but Doctor Sloper was not at home at the time. Catherine was with her aunt when a servant announced the young man's name. Mrs Penniman sent her niece into the parlour alone.

'This time it's for you – for you only,' she said.

So Catherine saw Mr Townsend alone, sitting with him in the front parlour, for more than an hour. He seemed more at home this time – making himself very comfortable and looking around with interest at the room and the furniture. His talk was light, easy and friendly. 'Tell me about yourself,' he said to her, with his charming smile.

Catherine had very little to tell, but she told him of her love of music and the theatre, and how she did not really enjoy reading. Morris Townsend agreed with her that books were boring – he had been to places that people had written about, and they were not at all as they had been described. He had also seen all the famous actors in London and Paris, but the actors were always like the writers – they were never true to real life. He liked everything to be natural. Suddenly he stopped, looking at Catherine with his smile.

'That's what I like you for; you are so natural,' he said. 'You see I am natural myself.'

He went on to talk about his great love of music and singing. 'I sing a little myself,' he added; 'some day I will show you. Not today, but some other time.'

And then he got up to go. He had perhaps talked more about himself than about Catherine, but the truth was that Catherine had not noticed. She was thinking only that 'some other time' had a delightful sound. It seemed to suggest many more meetings in the future.

Catherine felt it was her duty to tell her father that Mr Morris Townsend had called again – though it made her feel ashamed and uncomfortable. She announced the fact very suddenly, as soon as the Doctor came into the house, and then immediately tried to leave the room. Her father stopped her just as she reached the door.

'Well, my dear, did he ask you to marry him today?' the Doctor said.

Catherine had no answer ready. She wanted to be amused, as her father was amused, but she also wanted to be a little sharp, so that he would not ask the question again. She did not like it – it made her unhappy.

'Perhaps he will do it next time,' she said, with a little laugh; and she quickly got out of the room.

The Doctor stood staring. He wondered whether his

daughter was serious, and decided to find out more about this handsome young man. The next time he saw his sister Elizabeth, he asked her about Morris Townsend.

'Lavinia has already been to ask me about him,' Mrs Almond said.

'What did you tell her?' the Doctor asked.

'What I tell you – that I know very little of him.'

'How disappointing for Lavinia,' said the Doctor. 'She would like him to have some romantic secret in his past. I hear that he is a distant cousin of Arthur Townsend.'

'Yes, though it seems that there are Townsends and Townsends – some rather better than others. Arthur's mother knows very little about him; only some story that he has been 'wild' in the past. I know his sister a little. Her name is Mrs Montgomery; she is a widow, with five children and not much money.'

'What is his profession?' asked the Doctor.

'He hasn't got any; he is looking for something. I believe he was once in the Navy.'

'Once? What is his age?'

'More than thirty, I think. Arthur told me that he inherited a little money – which is perhaps why he left the Navy – and that he spent it all in a few years. He travelled all over the world, lived in foreign countries, amused himself. He has recently come back to America, and he told Arthur that he now wants to start his life seriously.'

'Is he serious about Catherine, then?'

'I don't see why you are surprised,' said Mrs Almond. 'It

seems to me that you have never been fair to Catherine. You must remember that she will one day have thirty thousand dollars a year.'

The Doctor looked at his sister for a moment: 'I see that you remember it.'

Mrs Almond blushed. 'I don't mean that is the only good thing about her; I simply mean that it is important. You seem to think that nobody will ever want to marry her.'

'Why should I think differently, Elizabeth?' the Doctor said. 'How many young men have come courting Catherine, even with her expected fortune? None – which is why Lavinia is so charmed that there is now a lover in the house. It is the first time.'

'I think young men are rather afraid of Catherine,' said the Doctor's wiser sister. 'She seems older than they are – she is so large, and she dresses so richly. An older, more experienced man would recognize all the good things in her character, and would find her delightful.'

'And Mr Townsend? What are his reasons for courting Catherine? Is he sincere in liking her?'

'It is very possible that he is sincere. Lavinia is sure of it.'

Doctor Sloper thought for a moment. 'If he does not work, what are his means?'

'I have no idea. He lives with his sister and her children on Second Avenue.'

'A widow, with five children? Do you mean he lives *upon* her?'

Mrs Almond looked at her brother a little impatiently.

'Why not ask Mrs Montgomery yourself?' she said.

'Perhaps I will,' said the Doctor.

⌒⚬⚬⚬⚬⌒

Doctor Sloper was more amused than annoyed by the idea of Mr Townsend courting his daughter. He was quite willing to believe the best of the young man. And if he was a sincere, honest man, it did not matter if he was poor, since Catherine had no need of a rich husband.

'The next time he comes,' he told Mrs Penniman, 'you must invite him to dinner.'

Mrs Penniman was happy to pass on her brother's invitation, which Morris Townsend accepted, and the dinner was arranged. Two or three other people were invited as well, and although Doctor Sloper talked very little to the young man during the meal, he watched him carefully. At the end of the meal, when the ladies had gone up to the parlour, leaving the men to their drinking, the Doctor gave him some wine and asked him several questions. Morris Townsend was happy to talk, and the Doctor sat quietly, watching his bright, handsome face.

'He is clever, a good talker, and very self-confident,' Catherine's father thought. 'And he dresses very well. But I don't think I like him.'

The Doctor, however, kept his thoughts to himself.

Later, when the men joined the ladies in the parlour, Morris Townsend went over to Catherine, who was standing before the fire in her red evening dress.

'Your father doesn't like me,' said the young man.

*Although Dr Sloper talked very little to the young man,
he watched him carefully.*

'I don't see how you know,' said Catherine, blushing.

'I can feel these things. You ask him and you will see.'

'I would rather not ask him, if there is any danger of his
saying what you think.'

Morris gave her a sad little smile. 'So you will allow him to
say things against me, and not tell him he is wrong?'

'I never argue with him,' said Catherine. 'And he won't say

anything against you. He doesn't know you enough.'

Morris Townsend gave a loud laugh, and Catherine began to blush again.

'I shall never talk about you,' she said.

'That is very well; but I would prefer you to say that it doesn't matter what your father thinks.'

'But it would matter! I couldn't say that!' the girl cried.

He stared at her, smiling a little, and just for a moment there was an impatient look in those fine eyes. But he spoke softly and sadly. 'Then I must try to make him like me.'

The next time the Doctor visited Mrs Almond, he told her that he had now met Morris Townsend.

'He is certainly a fine-looking young man,' he said.

'But what do you think of him, as a father?' Mrs Almond asked. 'Lavinia tells me that Catherine is in love.'

'Well, she must stop being in love. He is not a gentleman. He is extremely charming, and completely insincere.'

'You have decided very quickly,' said Mrs Almond.

'Not at all. I have been studying people for a lifetime, and am now quite able to make a judgement in a single evening.'

'Very possibly you are right. But the thing is for Catherine to see it.'

'I will give her a pair of glasses!' said the Doctor.

4
Morris Townsend looks for a position

If it were true that Catherine was in love, she was certainly very quiet about it. She had told Morris Townsend that she would not mention him to her father, and so she said nothing about Morris's continued visits. It was only polite, of course, for Morris to visit after the dinner at Washington Square, and only natural for him to continue visiting.

These visits had quickly become the most important thing in Catherine's life. She was very happy. She did not yet know what the future would bring, and she was too modest to expect anything. She was just grateful for the present – the sound of his voice, the words he spoke to her, the expression of his face.

Doctor Sloper suspected Morris Townsend's visits, and noticed how quiet Catherine had become.

'What is going on in this house?' he asked his sister.

'Going on, Austin?' said Mrs Penniman.

'Why haven't you told me that Mr Morris Townsend is coming to the house four or five times a week? I am away all day, and I see nothing.'

Mrs Penniman thought for a moment. 'Dear Austin,' she said at last, 'I cannot tell a secret.'

'Whose secret? Catherine's? Mr Townsend's? If it is his, I think it is extremely foolish of you to have secrets with young men. You don't know where they will lead you.'

'I don't know what you mean,' said Mrs Penniman. 'I take a great interest in Mr Townsend; I don't hide that. But that is all.'

'It is quite enough. And what do you find so interesting about Mr Townsend? His good looks?'

'His misfortunes, Austin. I cannot tell you his story, but he would tell it to you himself, if he thought you would listen to him kindly.'

The Doctor gave a laugh. 'I shall ask him very kindly to leave Catherine alone.'

'Catherine probably says kinder things to him than that!'

'Has she said that she loved him? – do you mean that?'

Mrs Penniman stared at the floor. 'She doesn't talk to me about him. I think she is very happy; that is all I can say.'

'Townsend wants to marry her – is that what you mean?'

'He admires Catherine greatly,' said Mrs Penniman. 'And he says the most charming things about her.'

'And these misfortunes that you refuse to tell me about – did they make him poor?'

'It is a long story,' said Mrs Penniman, 'and all I can say is that he has been wild in the past. But he has paid for it.'

The Doctor smoked his cigar in silence, then said, 'I am told he lives with his sister, and does nothing for himself.'

'He is looking very seriously for a position,' said Mrs Penniman. 'He hopes every day to find one.'

'Exactly. He is looking for it here, over there in the front parlour – the position of husband of a weak woman with a large fortune. That would suit him perfectly.'

Mrs Penniman got up and looked at her brother a little angrily. 'My dear Austin,' she said, 'you are making a great mistake if you think that Catherine is a weak woman!' And with this she walked away.

⸻⁂⸻

The family in Washington Square spent every Sunday evening at Mrs Almond's house. On the Sunday after his conversation with Mrs Penniman, Doctor Sloper went off to another room to talk to his brother-in-law about business. He came back later to find that Morris Townsend had arrived, and was sitting on a sofa beside Catherine. There were several friends of the family present, and it was easy for the two young people to sit and talk privately. The Doctor saw at once, however, that his daughter was painfully conscious that he was watching her. She sat very still, with her eyes down, blushing deeply.

Doctor Sloper felt so sorry for her that he turned his eyes away. 'Poor Catherine,' he thought. 'It must be very nice for her to have a beautiful young man court her. Perhaps I should give him another chance.'

A little later, when Morris Townsend was standing alone, the Doctor crossed the room towards him. The young man looked at him, with a little smile.

'He's amazingly conceited!' thought the Doctor. Then he said, 'I am told you are looking for a position.'

'Yes, I should like some work,' Morris Townsend replied. 'But I fear that I have no special talents.'

'You are too modest,' said the Doctor. 'I know nothing of

you except what I see; but I see by your face that you are extremely intelligent.'

'Ah,' Townsend said, 'I don't know what to answer when you say that. You advise me, then, not to give up hope?'

The question seemed to have a double meaning, and the Doctor looked at him for a moment before he answered. 'No young man should ever give up hope. If he does not succeed in one thing, he can try another.'

Morris Townsend stared down at his shoes. 'Were you kindly suggesting a position for me?' he then asked, looking up and smiling.

This annoyed the Doctor, and he paused for a moment. Then he said, 'I sometimes hear of possibilities. How would you feel, for example, about leaving New York?'

'*You advise me, then, not to give up hope?' said Morris.*

'I am afraid I could not do that. I must find my fortune in this city. You see,' added Morris Townsend, 'I have responsibilities here. I have a sister who depends on me.'

'Family feeling is very important,' said Doctor Sloper. 'I often think there is not enough of it in our city. I think I have heard of your sister.'

'It is possible, but I doubt it. She lives so very quietly.'

'As quietly, you mean,' the Doctor went on, with a short laugh, 'as a lady may do with several small children.'

'I help with my little nephews and nieces,' said Morris Townsend. 'I am their teacher.'

'That is very good, but it is not a career.'

'It won't make my fortune,' agreed the young man.

Later in the evening the Doctor spoke to Mrs Almond. 'I should like to see his sister,' he said. 'Mrs Montgomery. Mr Townsend tells me he teaches her children.'

'I will try and arrange it for you,' said Mrs Almond. 'I must say, he doesn't look in the least like a schoolteacher.'

And when Morris Townsend spoke to Catherine again later, he did not sound like a schoolteacher either.

'Will you meet me somewhere tomorrow?' he murmured. 'I have something particular to say to you – very particular.'

'Can't you come to the house? Can't you say it there?' Catherine asked, lifting her frightened eyes.

Townsend shook his head sadly. 'I cannot enter your doors again. Your father has insulted me.'

'Insulted you?'

'He dislikes me because I am poor.'

'Oh, you are wrong – you misunderstood him,' said Catherine, getting up from her chair.

'He laughed at me for having no position. I took it quietly; but only because he belongs to you.'

'I don't know what he thinks,' said Catherine. 'I am sure he means to be kind. You must not be too proud.'

'I will be proud only of you, my dearest,' said Morris, and Catherine blushed. 'Will you meet me tomorrow evening in the garden in the Square? It is very quiet there – no one will see us.'

Catherine hesitated. Young ladies did not go out alone in the evenings to meet young men in gardens. 'I am not – not very brave,' she said.

'Ah, then, if you are afraid, what shall we do?'

She hesitated again; then at last said, 'You must come to the house. I am not afraid of that.'

'I would rather meet in the Square,' the young man said. 'You know how empty it is, often. No one will see us.'

'I don't care who sees us. But leave me now.'

He left her. He had got what he wanted.

⸎

Catherine met the young man next day in the place she had chosen – among the elegant furniture of a New York parlour. Mrs Penniman, as usual, left the two young people alone to enjoy their romantic meeting.

'We must decide what to do,' said Morris.

He had already, on earlier visits, told Catherine that he loved her. He had put his arm around her and taken kisses, which had made her heart beat very fast. She felt deeply, wonderfully happy, but she was also confused and a little frightened. After Morris had kissed her, on his last visit, she had begged him to go away, to let her think. She felt his kisses on her lips for a long time afterwards, and she could not think clearly at all. What would she do if, as she feared, her father told her that he did not like Morris Townsend?

Today, however, when Morris spoke about deciding something, she felt that it was the truth, and said simply:

'We must do our duty; we must speak to my father. I will do it tonight; you must do it tomorrow.'

'It is very good of you to do it first,' Morris answered. 'The young man – the happy lover – usually does that.'

'You must promise to be gentle with my father.'

'I shall try,' Morris promised. 'But do you know what your father will say? He will tell you I want your money.'

'Oh!' murmured Catherine, softly. 'How wrong he is!'

Morris gave her a fond little kiss.

'I shall tell him that he is wrong,' said Catherine.

'He will argue with you.'

Catherine looked at her lover for a minute, and then she said, 'I shall persuade him. But I am glad we shall be rich.'

Morris turned away. 'No, it's a misfortune,' he said. 'It is from that our problems will come.'

'If it is the worst misfortune, we are not so unhappy. I will persuade him, and after that we shall be very glad we have money.'

Morris listened to these sensible words in silence. 'You

28

must speak for me on this; I cannot do it myself.'

Catherine, too, was silent for a while. She looked at Morris, who was staring out of the window. 'Morris,' she said, suddenly, 'are you very sure you love me?'

He turned round, and came to her at once. 'My own dearest, can you doubt it?'

'I have only known it five days,' she said, 'but now it seems to me something I could not live without.'

'You will never need to try.' He gave a gentle laugh. Then he added, 'There is something you must tell me, too.' Catherine had closed her eyes, and kept them closed. 'You must tell me,' Morris went on, 'that if your father is against me, you will still be faithful.'

Catherine opened her eyes and stared at him. She could give no better promise than what he read there.

5
Doctor Sloper decides

Catherine listened for her father when he came in that evening, and she heard him go to his study. She sat quiet, though her heart was beating fast, for nearly half an hour; then she went and knocked on his door. On entering the room, she found him in his chair beside the fire, with a cigar and the evening paper.

'I have something to say to you,' she began very gently.

'I shall be happy to hear it, my dear,' said her father. He

29

waited, looking at her, while she stared silently at the fire.

'I am engaged to be married!' Catherine said at last.

The Doctor did not show how surprised he was. 'You are right to tell me,' he said. 'And who is the happy man?'

'Mr Morris Townsend.' As she said her lover's name, Catherine looked at him. Then she looked back at the fire.

'When did this happen?' the Doctor asked.

'I am engaged to be married!' Catherine said at last.

'This afternoon – two hours ago.'

'Was Mr Townsend here?'

'Yes, father, in the front parlour.' She was very glad that she did not have to tell him her engagement had taken place in the garden of the Square.

Her father was silent for a moment. 'Why did Mr Townsend not tell me? It is his duty to speak to me first.'

'He means to tell you tomorrow.'

The Doctor smoked his cigar for a while. 'You have gone very fast,' he said, at last.

'Yes,' Catherine answered, simply. 'I think we have.'

Her father looked at her for a moment. 'I'm not surprised that Mr Townsend likes you. You are so simple and good.'

'I don't know why; but he does like me. I am sure of that. And I like him very much.'

'But you have known him a very short time, my dear.'

'Oh,' said Catherine, 'it doesn't take long to like a person – once you have begun.'

'Of course you are no longer a little girl.'

'I feel very old – and very wise,' said Catherine, smiling.

'I am afraid that you will soon feel older and wiser. I don't like your engagement.'

'Oh,' said Catherine, softly, getting up from her chair.

'No, my dear. I am sorry to give you pain; but I don't like it. Why didn't you speak to me first?'

Catherine hesitated a moment. Then she said, 'I was afraid you didn't like Mr Townsend.'

'You were quite right. I don't like him.'

'Dear father, you don't know him,' said Catherine gently. She remembered Morris's warning. 'You think he is only interested in my fortune.'

Doctor Sloper looked up at her, with his cold, reasonable eyes. 'I am not accusing Mr Townsend of that. You are an honest, kind-hearted girl, and there is nothing impossible in an intelligent young man loving you for yourself. But the main thing that we know about this young man is that he has spent his own fortune in amusing himself. There is good reason to believe that he would spend yours, too.'

'That is not the only thing we know about him. He is kind, and generous, and true,' said poor Catherine. She was not used to arguing, and her voice trembled a little. 'And the fortune he spent was very small.'

The Doctor stood up. He held her for a moment and kissed her. 'You won't think me cruel?' he said.

The question filled Catherine with fear, but she said, 'No, dear father; because if you knew how I feel, you would be so kind, so gentle.'

'Yes, I think I know how you feel,' the Doctor said. 'I will be very kind – be sure of that. And I will see Mr Townsend tomorrow. Meanwhile, do not tell anyone you are engaged.'

The next afternoon the Doctor stayed at home, waiting for Morris Townsend's visit. When the young man arrived, Doctor Sloper began at once.

'Catherine told me yesterday what has been going on between you,' he said. 'I am very surprised. It was only the other day that you first met my daughter.'

'It was not long ago, certainly,' said Morris. 'My interest in Miss Sloper began the first time I saw her.'

'Did it not start before you met her?' the Doctor asked.

Morris looked at him. 'I had certainly already heard that she was a charming girl.'

'Naturally, you will speak well of her,' said the Doctor. 'But that is not the only thing that is necessary. I told Catherine yesterday that I did not like her engagement.'

'She told me, and I was very sorry to hear it. I am greatly disappointed,' said Morris, looking at the floor.

'Did you really expect me to say I was delighted?'

'Oh no! I had an idea you didn't like me.'

'What gave you that idea?'

'The fact that I am poor.'

'It is certainly a fact I must consider,' said the Doctor. 'I do not dislike you, but you do not appear to be a suitable husband for my daughter, who is a weak young woman with a large fortune.'

Morris listened politely. 'I don't think Miss Sloper is a weak woman,' he said.

'I have known my child twenty years, and you have known her six weeks. But whether she is weak or not, you are still a man without a profession, and without money.'

'Yes, that is *my* weakness! You think I only want your daughter's money.'

'I don't say that. I only say that you are the wrong kind of man to marry my daughter.'

'A man who loves and admires her deeply – is that the

wrong kind of man?' Morris said, with his handsome smile. 'I don't care about her fortune. Not in any way.'

'Fine words,' said the Doctor; 'but you are still the wrong kind of man.'

'You think I would spend her money – is that it?'

'Yes, I'm afraid I do think that.'

'It is true that I was foolish when I was younger,' said Morris, 'but I have changed now. I spent my own fortune, because it was my own. That does not mean I would spend Miss Sloper's fortune. I would take good care of it.'

'Taking too much care would be as bad as taking too little. Both ways would give Catherine an unhappy life.'

'I think you are very unjust!' said the young man.

'I can understand that you think that.'

'Do you want to make your daughter miserable?'

'I accept that she will think I am cruel for a year.'

'A year!' said Morris, with a laugh.

'For a lifetime, then. She will be miserable either way – with you or without you.'

Here at last Morris became angry. 'You are not polite, sir!' he cried.

'I'm afraid that is your fault – you argue too much. I cannot accept you as a son-in-law, and I shall advise Catherine to give you up, which she will do.'

'Are you sure that she will give me up?' asked Morris. 'I don't think she will. She has gone too far . . . to stop.'

The Doctor stared at him coldly for a moment.

'I will say no more, sir,' said Morris, and he left the room.

When the Doctor told Mrs Almond about his meeting with Morris Townsend, she thought that he had perhaps been too hard on the young man.

'Lavinia thinks I am being very cruel,' said the Doctor.

'And how is Catherine taking it?' said Mrs Almond.

'Very quietly. There have been no noisy tears, or anything of that kind.'

'I am very sorry for Catherine,' Mrs Almond said. 'Now she will have to choose between her father and her lover.'

'I am sorry for her too,' said the Doctor. 'It is just possible, of course, that I have made the greatest mistake of my life. So I shall go and visit Mr Townsend's sister, who will almost certainly tell me I have done the right thing.'

The visit was arranged for a few days later, and at the appointed time the Doctor arrived at a little house on Second Avenue, where Mrs Montgomery received him in a small front parlour.

She was a little woman, with fair hair, and seemed rather alarmed by a visit from such a fine gentleman as Doctor Sloper. He explained the situation, but Mrs Montgomery was at first a little unwilling to talk about her brother.

'I can understand,' said the Doctor, 'that it is difficult for you to say unpleasant things about your own brother, but if my daughter married him, her happiness would depend on whether he was a good man or not.'

'Yes, I see that,' murmured Mrs Montgomery.

'And I must remind you,' said the Doctor, 'that after my

death Catherine will have thirty thousand dollars a year.'

Mrs Montgomery listened with wide eyes. 'Your daughter will be very rich,' she said, softly.

'Exactly. But if Catherine marries without my consent, she will have only the ten thousand dollars she inherited from her mother. She won't get a penny from me. I will be happy to inform Mr Townsend of that.'

'Your daughter will be very rich,' said Mrs Montgomery softly.

Mrs Montgomery thought for a while. 'Why do you dislike Morris so much?' she asked at last, looking up.

'I don't dislike him – he is a charming young man. But I dislike him as a son-in-law, who must take care of my daughter. She is so soft, so weak. A bad husband could make her very miserable indeed, because she is not clever enough or strong enough to fight her own battles. That is why I have come to you. You may not agree with me, of course; you may want to tell me to go away, but I think that your brother is selfish and lazy, and I should like to know if I am right.'

She looked at him in surprise. 'But how did you find out that he was selfish?' she said. 'He hides it so well.' Then she turned her head away, and the Doctor saw tears in her eyes.

He waited for a moment, then said suddenly, 'Your brother has made you very unhappy, hasn't he? Tell me, do you give him money?'

'Yes, I have given him money,' said Mrs Montgomery.

'And you have very little money yourself, and also five children to take care of, I believe.'

'It is true that I am very poor,' she said.

'Your brother tells me,' said the Doctor, 'that he helps you with your children – he is their teacher.'

Mrs Montgomery stared for a moment, then said quickly, 'Oh yes; he teaches them – Spanish.'

The Doctor laughed. 'That must be a great help to you! So,' he went on, 'I see that I was right. Your brother lives on you, takes your money, and is extremely selfish.'

There were tears again in Mrs Montgomery's eyes. 'But he

is still my brother,' she said, her voice trembling a little. 'You must not believe that his character is bad.'

The Doctor spoke more gently. 'I am sorry that I have upset you. It's all for my poor Catherine. You must know her, and then you will see.' He stood up to go.

Mrs Montgomery also stood up. 'I should like to know your daughter,' she answered; and then, very suddenly – 'Don't let her marry him!'

And Doctor Sloper went away with these words ringing in his ears.

6
Catherine tries to be good

The Doctor was surprised, and even a little disappointed, to see that Catherine did not appear to be angry or upset about what had happened. He wanted to be kind to her, but she did not seem to want or need his kindness.

'I am glad I have such a good daughter,' he said, after several days had passed.

'I am trying to be good,' she answered, turning away.

'If you have anything to say about Mr Townsend, I shall be happy to listen.'

'Thank you,' said Catherine. 'I have nothing to say at present.'

He never asked her whether she had seen Morris again. She had, in fact, not seen him; she had only written him a long letter. 'I am in great trouble,' she wrote. 'Do not doubt my love for you, but let me wait a little and think.' But her thoughts were not at all clear. She could not really believe that her father would change his mind about Morris; she just hoped that in some mysterious way the situation would get better. Meanwhile, she felt she must try to be a good daughter, to be patient, and to search for a peaceful way out of their difficulty.

She received no help from her aunt in this search. Mrs Penniman was enjoying all the excitement of the romance and had no sensible advice to offer poor Catherine. 'You must act, my dear,' she said. 'The important thing is to act.'

Mrs Penniman had also written to Morris, and had arranged to meet him secretly in a café on the other side of the city. She had not told her niece about this meeting, and so was a little embarrassed when Morris arrived and asked if she had a message for him from Catherine.

'Not exactly a message,' she said. 'I didn't ask her for one. But she will be true to you – until death.'

'Oh, I hope it won't come to that,' said Morris.

'My brother will not listen to argument.'

'Do you mean he won't change his mind?'

Mrs Penniman was silent for a moment, then she smiled at Morris. 'Marry Catherine first, and tell him afterwards!' she cried. 'That is the way I see it: a secret marriage.'

The young man stared at her. 'Do you advise me to do that? To marry her without her father's consent?'

She was a little frightened, but went on, 'If you marry

Catherine, you will show my brother that he has been wrong about you. He will see that it is not just because you like – you like the money.'

Morris hesitated, then said, 'But I *do* like the money.'

'But you don't like it more than Catherine. And when he realizes that, he will think it is his duty to help you.'

Morris looked for some moments at the floor. At last he

'Marry Catherine first, and tell him afterwards!' Mrs Penniman cried.

looked up and said, 'Do you think there is already a will leaving money to Catherine?'

'I suppose so – even doctors must die,' she replied.

'And you believe he would certainly change it – if I married Catherine?'

'Yes, but then he would change it back again.'

'But I can't depend on that,' said Morris.

'Do you want to *depend* on it?' Mrs Penniman asked.

He blushed a little. 'I do not want to injure Catherine.'

'You must not be afraid! Be afraid of nothing, and everything will go well.'

Mrs Penniman told Catherine that evening that she had had a meeting with Morris Townsend, and for almost the first time in her life Catherine felt angry.

'Why did you see him? I don't think it was right.'

'I was so sorry for him – and you wouldn't see him, my dear,' said Aunt Lavinia.

'I have not seen him because my father has forbidden it,' Catherine said, very simply.

This annoyed Mrs Penniman and she began to read the evening newspaper, so that Catherine would have to ask her about her meeting with Morris. But it was several minutes before Catherine finally spoke. 'What did he say?' she asked.

'He said he is ready to marry you any day.'

Catherine made no answer to this, and after a few minutes Mrs Penniman added that Morris looked very tired.

Catherine got up from her seat and went to the fire.

Mrs Penniman hesitated for a moment. 'He said he was

41

afraid of only one thing – that you would be afraid.'

The girl turned very quickly. 'Afraid of what?'

'Afraid of your father.'

Catherine turned back to the fire again. After a pause, she said, 'I *am* afraid of my father.'

Mrs Penniman got up quickly from her chair and went to her niece. 'Are you going to give him up, then?'

For some time Catherine stared at the fire and did not move. Then she lifted her head and looked at her aunt. 'Why do you make it so difficult for me?' she said. 'I don't think you understand or that you know me. You had better not have any more meetings with Mr Townsend. I don't think it is right. My father wouldn't like it, if he knew.'

'And you will inform him – is that what you mean? Well, I am not afraid of my brother. But I shall not try to help again – you are too ungrateful. I am disappointed, but your father will not be. Good night.' And with this Mrs Penniman went off to her room.

ΘSSS∼

Catherine sat alone by the parlour fire, lost in her thoughts, for more than an hour. She felt that to displease her father was a terrible thing, but she had made a plan and must go on with it. Her father was in his study, and it was eleven o'clock when she finally knocked on his door. Even when he answered her, she was too afraid to go in. After a while he came and opened the door for her.

'What's the matter?' asked the Doctor. 'You are standing there like a ghost!'

She went into the room, and her father looked at her for a few moments, waiting for her to speak. He then went back to his writing desk and sat down, turning his back on his daughter. At last she began:

'You told me that if I had something more to say about Mr Townsend, you would be glad to listen to it.'

'Exactly, my dear,' said the Doctor, not turning round.

'I would like to see him again.'

'To say goodbye?' asked the Doctor.

'No, father, not that; at least not for ever.'

'You have not finished with him, then?'

'No,' said Catherine. 'I have asked him to – to wait.'

Her father, turning round in his chair, looked at her with his cold eyes, and she was afraid he was going to be angry.

'You are a dear, faithful child,' he said, at last. 'Come here to your father.' And he got up, holding his hands out towards her.

The words were a surprise, and they gave her great happiness. She went to him, and he put his arm round her gently, and kissed her. After this he said, 'Do you wish to make me very happy?'

'I would like to – but I am afraid I can't,' Catherine answered. 'Do you want me to give him up?'

'Yes, I want you to give him up.'

He still held her, looking into her face. She looked away and they were both silent for a long time.

'You are happier than I am, father,' she said at last.

'I have no doubt that you are unhappy now. But it is better

43

to be unhappy for three months, than miserable for the rest of your life.'

'Yes, if that were true,' said Catherine.

'It is true, I am sure of that.' When she did not answer, he went on, 'Don't you believe that I want the best for your future? I know how bad men can be – how false.'

She moved away from him. 'He is not false! What has he done – what do you know?'

'He has never done anything, that is the problem – he is lazy and selfish and thinks only of himself.'

'Oh, father, don't say bad things about him!' she cried.

'No, that would be a great mistake. You may do what you choose,' he added, turning away.

'If I see him again, will you forgive me?'

'No, I will not.'

'I only want to see him once – to tell him to wait.'

'To wait for what?'

'Until you know him better – until you consent.'

'I know him well enough, and I shall never consent.'

'But we can wait a long time,' said poor Catherine.

'Of course, you can wait until I die, if you like,' said the Doctor, quietly. 'Your engagement will have one delightful effect upon you; it will make you extremely impatient for my death. And think how impatient *he* will be, too.'

Catherine gave a cry of natural horror and stood staring. Her father's words had a terrible ugliness, and she did not know what to say. Suddenly, however, an idea came to her.

'If I don't marry before your death, I will not after,' she

said. 'But I think that one day Morris might persuade you.'

'I shall never speak to him again. I dislike him too much,' said the Doctor. 'And you can tell **Mr** Townsend when you see him again that if you marry without my consent, I will not leave you a penny of my money. That will interest him more than anything else you can tell him.'

She looked at her father, and her eyes filled with tears.

'I think I will see him, then,' she murmured.

'Exactly as you choose. But if you see him, you will be an ungrateful, cruel child; and you will give your old father the greatest pain of his life.'

The tears then ran down Catherine's face, and she moved towards her father with a little cry. But he only took her by the arm, went to the door, and opened it for her to go out.

After she had left, he walked around his study for a while, a little annoyed but also amused. 'My word,' he said to himself. 'I believe she will go on with it.' He looked forward to seeing what would happen next.

7
Catherine decides

The next day Doctor Sloper called Mrs Penniman into his study. 'I don't want Catherine, or you,' he said coldly, 'to see young Townsend again. And I expect you to obey me.'

'Do you wish to murder your child?' Mrs Penniman asked.

'No. I wish to make her live and be happy.'

Catherine moved towards her father with a little cry.

'You will kill her: she had a terrible night.'

'She won't die of one bad night, nor of several.'

It was true that Catherine had had a terrible, sleepless night. But, though her heart was breaking, she tried not to show her pain to the world. Mrs Penniman was very disappointed to see that there were no tears in her niece's eyes when she came down to breakfast.

That afternoon Catherine wrote to Morris, and the next day he came into the front parlour and stood before her. She thought that he looked more beautiful than ever.

'Why have you made me wait so long?' he asked. 'Every hour has seemed like years. Have you decided whether you will keep me or give me up?'

'Oh, Morris,' she cried, 'I never thought of giving you up!'

'What, then, were you waiting for?'

'I thought my father might – might look at it differently. But he – he looks at it still in the same way.'

'Then why have you sent for me?'

'Because I wanted to see you,' cried Catherine.

Morris watched her for a moment. 'Will you marry me tomorrow?' he asked, suddenly.

'Tomorrow?'

'Next week, then – any time in the next month.'

'Isn't it better to wait?' said Catherine.

'To wait for what?'

She did not know for what, but she felt afraid. 'Until we have thought about it a little more.'

He shook his head sadly. 'I thought you had been thinking

about it these three weeks. Do you want to go on doing that for five years? My poor girl,' he added, 'you are not faithful to me.'

Catherine blushed, and her eyes filled with tears. 'Oh, how can you say that?' she murmured.

'You must take me or leave me,' said Morris. 'You can't please your father *and* me. You must choose between us.'

'I have chosen you,' she said.

'Then marry me next week!'

She stood staring at him. 'Isn't there any other way?'

'None that I know of.' He turned away, walked to the window and stood looking out. 'You are very afraid of your father,' he said at last.

'I suppose I must be,' she said simply.

'Your fear of him seems greater than your love for me.'

'Oh, Morris,' she said, going to him.

After a while she told Morris what her father had said. 'If I marry without his consent, I shall not inherit any of his fortune. He told me to tell you that. He seemed to think—'

Morris blushed angrily. 'What did he seem to think?'

'That it would make a difference.'

'It *will* make a difference – in many things. But it will not change my love for you.'

'We shall not want the money,' said Catherine. 'You know that I have my own fortune.'

Morris was silent for a while. 'Do you think that he will be cruel to you for ever? That he will never change his mind about disinheriting you?'

'If I marry you, he will think I am not good.'

'Then he will never forgive you!' cried Morris.

Catherine suddenly felt lonely and afraid. 'Oh, Morris,' she cried, putting her head on his shoulder, 'you must love me very much. I will marry you as soon as you want!'

'My dear good girl!' he cried, looking down at her. She had given him her promise, but he was not quite sure what he would do with it.

⸎

For about a week, life in Washington Square continued much as before, and Doctor Sloper waited to see what would happen. He told his sister Elizabeth that he had never expected Catherine to give him so much excitement.

'It is not very kind of you,' said Mrs Almond, 'to find amusement in your daughter's situation.'

'I will take her to Europe,' said the Doctor, 'to give her some new ideas.'

'She won't forget him in Europe.'

'He will forget her, then.'

Mrs Almond looked serious. 'Would you really like that?'

'Extremely,' said the Doctor.

Mrs Penniman, meanwhile, arranged another secret meeting with Morris Townsend outside a church. She had been a little alarmed by her brother's coldness towards her.

'I think you should wait for a while before you marry,' she told Morris. 'Wait until my brother is less angry.'

The young man was very annoyed. 'Last week you advised me to marry immediately!' he said. 'Catherine has already agreed to this, so what can I do?'

'Catherine loves you so much that you can do anything,' said Mrs Penniman. 'You can change your plans, this way or that way, and she will not be upset with you.'

Morris looked at her, but said nothing, and soon after that they parted.

Catherine, of course, knew nothing of her aunt's meeting with Morris, and she had not spoken to her father since the evening she went to see him in his study. At last, however, she told him that she had seen Morris Townsend again.

'I think we shall marry – before very long,' she said.

The Doctor looked at her coldly from head to foot. 'Why do you tell me that? It is of no interest to me.'

Catherine turned away for a moment; there were tears in her eyes. 'Oh, father,' she cried, 'don't you care?'

'Not at all. Once you marry, it is the same to me when, or where, or why you do it.'

But the next day he spoke to her in a different way. 'Are you going to marry in the next four or five months?'

'I don't know, father,' said Catherine. 'It is not very easy for us to decide.'

'Wait, then, for six months, and meanwhile I will take you to Europe. I would very much like you to go.'

This sign of her father's interest in her gave Catherine great happiness. 'It would be delightful to go to Europe,' she said. But her happiness soon disappeared when she realized that she would not see Morris for several months.

Mrs Penniman was not invited, and she understood very

well why the Doctor had made this plan. 'He thinks the journey will make you forget Morris,' she told her niece.

Catherine could not decide whether to obey her father's wishes or not. She wrote to Morris and asked him to meet her in the Square. They met the next day, and during a long walk she told him about her father's invitation.

'He thinks I will forget you,' said Catherine.

'Well, my dear, perhaps you will. There are so many exciting things to see in Europe.'

'Please don't say that,' Catherine answered, gently. 'I am not interested in seeing Europe.'

'You should go,' said Morris. 'It will please your father, and perhaps he will forgive you and change his mind about disinheriting you.'

'And not get married for so long?'

'We can marry when you come back,' said Morris. 'You can buy your wedding clothes in Paris.'

⁂

They were away, in fact, for a year and during the first six months the name of Morris Townsend was not mentioned. The Doctor found much to interest him in Europe, but although Catherine was always quiet and obedient, she was, her father thought, a very unintelligent companion.

One day, at the end of the summer, they were walking together in a lonely valley in the mountains. It was beginning to get dark and the air was cold and sharp.

Suddenly the Doctor stopped and looked at Catherine.

'Have you given him up?' he asked.

The question was unexpected, but Catherine did not hesitate. 'No, father,' she answered.

He looked at her for some moments without speaking.

'Does he write to you?' he asked.

'Yes, about twice a month.'

The Doctor looked up and down the mountain, and said in a low voice, 'I am very angry.'

'I am sorry,' Catherine murmured. She felt lonely and frightened in this wild place.

'One day he will leave you,' said the Doctor. 'Alone and hungry, in a place like this. That's what he will do.'

'That's not true, father, and you should not say it,' she cried. 'It's not right!'

He shook his head slowly. 'No, it's not right, because you won't believe it. But it is true.'

Doctor Sloper did not speak of Morris again until the night before they sailed to New York. 'What are you going to do when you get home?' he asked suddenly.

'Do you mean about Mr Townsend?'

'About Mr Townsend.'

'We shall probably marry.'

'So you will go off with him as soon as you arrive?'

Catherine did not like the way he said this. 'I cannot tell you until we arrive,' she said.

'If I am going to lose my only child, I would like to know before it happens.'

'Oh, father! You will not lose me,' said Catherine.

'One day he will leave you,' said the Doctor.
'Alone and hungry, in a place like this.'

8
The last parting

Catherine did not 'go off' with Morris Townsend when she arrived in New York, but she did hear news of him from her aunt during her first evening home. In fact, while she had been away, Morris had been a frequent visitor in Washington Square, taking tea with Mrs Penniman and sitting in Doctor Sloper's study to smoke cigars. Mrs Almond had told her sister that she was behaving foolishly.

'You should not be so friendly with him, Lavinia,' she said. 'He will make Catherine a bad husband. If he marries her and she doesn't get Austin's money, he will hate her for his disappointment, and will be cruel to her. The poor girl will have a miserable life.'

But Mrs Penniman did not listen to her sister, and on Catherine's return she told her niece that she had taken good care of her lover while she had been away.

'And how is your father?' she asked. 'Has he changed his mind about disinheriting you?'

'No. In Europe I saw that I shall never change him,' said poor Catherine. 'I expect nothing from him now.'

'You have become very brave,' said Mrs Penniman, with a short laugh. 'I didn't advise you to give up your property.'

'Yes, I am braver than I was. I have changed in that way – I have changed very much. And it isn't my property. If Morris doesn't care about it, then I don't care either.'

Mrs Penniman hesitated. 'Perhaps he does care about it.'

'He cares about it because he doesn't want to injure me, but he knows that I am not afraid of that. Besides, I have my own money; we shall have enough to live well.'

The next day Morris Townsend came to visit Catherine.

'I am very glad you have come back,' he said. 'It makes me very happy to see you again.' He looked at her, smiling, from head to foot.

When Catherine saw his handsome face again, she found it hard to believe that this beautiful young man was hers. She was very happy, and without waiting for him to ask, she told Morris about her father.

'We must not expect his money now,' she said, 'and we must live without it.'

Morris sat looking and smiling. 'My poor, dear girl!' he cried.

'You must not be sad for me,' said Catherine.

Morris continued to smile, and then he got up and walked around the room. 'Let me talk to him,' he said. 'I want to prove to your father that he is wrong about me.'

'Please don't, Morris,' said Catherine sadly. 'We must ask nothing from him. I know he will never change.'

'Why not?'

She hesitated for a moment. 'He is not very fond of me,' she said slowly. 'And I think he despises me. I saw it, I felt it, in England, just before we left. It is because he is so fond of my mother, who died so many years ago. She was beautiful and very, very clever – he is always thinking of her. I am not at all like her; Aunt Penniman has told me that. Of course it isn't my fault, but neither is it his fault.'

'You are a strange family,' said Morris.

'Don't say that – don't say anything unkind,' Catherine said. 'You must be very kind to me now, because, Morris,' – here she hesitated – 'because I have done a lot for you.'

'Oh, I know that, my dear.'

'It has been terrible for me to feel so distant from my father – to feel that he despises me. I would be so miserable if I didn't love you. We must be very happy together! And, Morris, Morris, you must never despise me!'

This was an easy promise to make, and Morris made it. But for the moment he made no further promises.

❦

Doctor Sloper spoke to both his sisters soon after his return. He told Mrs Penniman that he would never accept Morris Townsend as a son-in-law, and he told Mrs Almond that he was now no longer amused by Catherine, only annoyed.

'She will never give Mr Townsend up,' said Mrs Almond.

'Then she will be very unhappy, and I can't prevent it.'

'Poor Catherine!' said Mrs Almond. 'We must be as kind to her as we can.'

Mrs Penniman arranged another secret meeting with Morris. They went for a long walk together, and she told him what the Doctor had said.

'He will never give us a penny,' said Morris angrily. After a pause, he added, 'I must give her up!'

Mrs Penniman was silent for a moment. Though she

56

thought of Morris as a son, she was also a little afraid of him. 'I think I understand you,' she said, gently. 'But my poor Morris, do you know how much she loves you?'

'No, I don't. I don't want to know.'

'It will be very hard for Catherine,' said Mrs Penniman.

'You must help her. The Doctor will help you; he will be delighted with the news.'

'He will say, "I always told you so!"'

Morris blushed bright red. 'I find this all very unpleasant,' he said. 'A true friend would try and make it easier for me.'

'Would you like me to tell her?' Mrs Penniman asked.

'You mustn't tell her, but you can—' He hesitated, trying to think what Mrs Penniman could do. 'You can explain that I don't want to come between her and her father.'

'Are you not going to come and see her again?'

'Oh no, I shall come again, but I want this business to end soon. I have been four times since she came back, and it's very hard work.'

'But you must have your last parting!' his companion cried. For Mrs Penniman the last parting between lovers was almost as romantic as the first meeting.

―❦―

Morris came to Washington Square again, without managing the last parting; and again and again. Catherine did not suspect anything was wrong, and Mrs Penniman was too frightened to say anything to her. During each visit the poor girl waited for Morris to name the day of their wedding. But he never stayed more than a few minutes, and seemed so uncomfortable that at last she became worried.

'Are you sick?' she asked him.

'I am not at all well,' he said. 'And I have to go away.'

'Go away? Where are you going, Morris?'

He looked at her, and for a second or two she was afraid of him. 'Will you promise not to be angry?' he said.

'Angry! – do I get angry?'

'I have to go away on business – to New Orleans.'

'What is your business? Your business is to be with me.'

He told her a long story about a chance he had to make a lot of money buying cotton, but Catherine took his arm in her two hands and spoke more violently than he had ever heard her speak before.

'You can go to New Orleans some other time. This isn't the moment to choose. We have waited too long already.'

'You said you would not be angry!' cried Morris. He got up to leave. 'Very well; we won't talk about it any more. I will do the business by letter.'

'You won't go?' said Catherine, looking at him.

Morris wanted to argue with her; it would make it easier for him to break away. 'You mustn't tell me what to do,' he said. 'Try and be calmer the next time I come.'

'When will you come again?'

'I will come next Saturday,' said Morris.

'Come tomorrow,' Catherine begged; 'I want you to come tomorrow. I will be very quiet.' Suddenly she felt very frightened, and did not want him to leave the room.

Morris kissed the top of her head. Catherine felt her heart

beat very fast. 'Will you promise to come tomorrow?'

'I said Saturday!' Morris answered, smiling. He tried to be angry at one moment, and smile at the next; it was all very difficult and unpleasant.

'Yes, Saturday, too,' she answered, trying to smile. 'But tomorrow first.' He was going to the door, and she went with him quickly.

'I am a busy man!' cried Morris.

His voice was so hard and unnatural that she turned away. He quickly put his hand on the door. But in a moment she was close to him again, murmuring, 'Morris, you are going to leave me.'

'Yes, for a little while. Until you are reasonable again.'

'I shall never be reasonable, in that way.' She tried to keep

'I am a busy man!' cried Morris.

him longer. 'Think of what I have done!' she cried. 'Morris, I have given up everything.'

'You shall have everything back.'

'You wouldn't say that if you didn't mean something. What is it? What has happened? What have I done? What has changed you?'

'I will write to you – that is better.'

'You won't come back!' she cried, tears running down her face.

'Dear Catherine,' he said, 'don't believe that. I promise you that you shall see me again.' And he managed to get away, and to close the door behind him.

⟨✦⟩

For many hours Catherine lay crying on the sofa. He had said he would return, but she had seen an expression on his face that she had never seen before. He had wanted to get away from her; he had been angry and cruel, and said strange things, with strange looks. She tried to believe that he would come back; she listened, hoping to hear his ring at the door, but he did not return, nor did he call or write the next day. On Saturday Catherine sent him a note. 'I don't understand,' she wrote. 'Morris, you are killing me!'

The pain in Cathcrine's heart was terrible, but she was desperate to hide from her father what had happened, so she tried very hard to be brave. She ate her meals, went on with her daily life as usual, and said nothing to anybody.

'I am afraid you are in trouble, my dear,' Mrs Penniman said to her. 'Can I do anything to help you?'

'I am not in any trouble, and do not need any help,' said
Catherine.

After a few days the Doctor, who had been watching in
silence, spoke to his sister Lavinia.

'The thing has happened – he has left her!'

'It seems to make you happy to see your daughter upset!'

'It does,' said the Doctor; 'because it shows I was right.'

The following afternoon Catherine went for a walk, and
returned to find Mrs Penniman waiting for her.

'Dear Catherine, you cannot pretend with me,' said her
aunt. 'I know everything. And it is better that you should
separate.'

'Separate? Who said we were going to separate?'

'Isn't it broken off?' asked Mrs Penniman.

'My engagement? Not at all!'

'I am sorry then. I have spoken too soon! But what has
happened between you?' said Mrs Penniman; 'because
something has certainly happened.'

'Nothing has happened. I love him more and more!'

Mrs Penniman was silent. 'I suppose that's why you went
to see him this afternoon.'

Catherine blushed. 'Yes, I did go to see him!' she cried. 'But
that's my own business!'

'Then we won't talk about it.' Mrs Penniman moved
towards the door, but stopped when Catherine cried out:

'Aunt Lavinia, where has he gone? At his house they said he
had left town. I asked no more questions; I was ashamed. Has
he gone to New Orleans?'

Mrs Penniman had not heard of the New Orleans plan, but she did not tell Catherine this. 'If you have agreed to separate,' she said, 'the further he goes away, the better.'

Catherine stared. 'Agreed? Has he agreed it with you?'

'He has sometimes asked for my advice.'

'Is it you, then, that has changed him?' Catherine cried. 'Is it you that has taken him from me? How could you be so cruel? What have I ever done to you?'

'You are a most ungrateful girl,' said Mrs Penniman. 'It was me who helped bring you together.'

'I wish he had never come to the house! That's better than this,' said poor Catherine. She was silent for a few minutes, then got up and walked around the room.

'Will you please tell me where he is?'

'I have no idea,' said Mrs Penniman.

'Will he stay away for ever?'

'Oh, for ever is a long time. Your father, perhaps, won't live for ever.'

Catherine stared at her aunt. 'He has planned it, then. He has broken it off, and given me up.'

'Only for the present, dear Catherine.'

'He has left me alone,' said Catherine, shaking her head slowly. 'I don't believe it!'

Two days later Catherine received a long letter from Morris. It explained that he was in Philadelphia, and that he would be away on business for a long time. He said he would find it impossible to forget her, but he did not want to come between her and her rightful fortune. It was his dearest wish that she should have a happy and peaceful life, and he hoped that they would one day meet as friends.

The pain that this letter gave Catherine lasted for a long time, but she was too proud to say anything about it to her aunt or her father. Doctor Sloper waited a week, before coming one morning into the back parlour, where he found his daughter alone. She was sitting with some sewing work, and he came and stood in front of her. He was going out, and had his hat on.

'I would be grateful if you would tell me when you plan to leave my house,' he said.

Catherine looked at him, with a long silent stare. 'I shall not go away!' she said.

The Doctor looked surprised. 'Has he left you?'

'I have broken off my engagement.'

'Broken it off?'

'I have asked him to leave New York, and he has gone away for a long time.'

The Doctor did not believe this, and he was disappointed at losing the chance to say that he had been right.

'How does he like your sending him away?' he asked.

'I don't know!' said Catherine.

'You mean you don't care? You are rather cruel, after playing with him for so long.'

The Doctor had his revenge, after all.

'*I shall not go away!*' Catherine said.

9
Morris returns

No one ever learnt the truth about the end of Catherine's engagement. Catherine never spoke about it, keeping her secret even from Mrs Almond, who was very kind to her after Morris Townsend had left New York.

'I am delighted that Catherine did not marry him,' Mrs Almond said to her brother, 'but I wish you would be more gentle with her, Austin. Surely you feel sorry for her?'

'Why should I feel sorry for her? She has had a lucky escape. And I suspect that she has not really given him up at all. I think it is quite possible that they have made an arrangement to wait; and when I am dead, he will come back, and then she will marry him.'

Outwardly, Catherine seemed unchanged, but the fact was that she had been deeply hurt. Nothing could ever take away the pain that Morris had caused her, and nothing could ever make her feel towards her father as she had felt when she was younger.

Many years passed; years in which Catherine received more than a few offers of marriage. She refused them all, and though the name Morris Townsend was never mentioned in Washington Square, Doctor Sloper still suspected that his daughter was secretly waiting for him. 'If she is not, why doesn't she marry?' he asked himself. This idea grew stronger as he got older, and one day the Doctor said something to his daughter that surprised her very much.

'I would like you to promise me something before I die.'

'Why do you talk about dying?' she asked.

'Because I am sixty-eight years old. And I will die one day. Promise me you will never marry Morris Townsend.'

For some moments she said nothing. 'Why do you speak of him?' she asked at last.

'Because he has been in New York, and at your cousin Marian's house. Your Aunt Elizabeth tells me that he is looking for another wife – I don't know what happened to the first one. He has grown fat and bald, and he has not made his fortune.'

'Fat and bald'; these words sounded strange to Catherine. Her memory was of the most beautiful young man in the world. 'I don't think you understand,' she said. 'I almost never think of Mr Townsend. But I can't promise that.'

The Doctor was silent for a minute. 'I ask you for a particular reason. I am changing my will.'

Very few things made Catherine angry, but these words brought back painful memories from the past. She felt that her father was pushing her too far.

'I can't promise,' she simply repeated.

'Please explain.'

'I can't explain,' said Catherine, 'and I can't promise.'

A year later Doctor Sloper died after a three-week illness. The will he had changed shortly before his death now left Catherine only a fifth of his property. Mrs Penniman thought that this was cruel and unjust, but Catherine was neither surprised nor unhappy about the new will. 'I like it very much,' she told her aunt.

⌒*sss*⌒

Catherine and Mrs Penniman continued to live in the house in Washington Square. On a warm evening in July, a year after Doctor Sloper's death, the two ladies sat together at an open window, looking out on the quiet square.

'Catherine,' said Mrs Penniman. 'I have something to say that will surprise you. I have seen Morris Townsend.'

Catherine remained very still for some moments. 'I hope he was well,' she said at last.

'I don't know. He would like very much to see you.'

'I would rather not see him,' said Catherine, quickly.

'I was afraid you would say that,' said Mrs Penniman. 'I met him at Marian's house, and they are so afraid you will meet him there. I think that's why he goes. He very much wants to see you.' Catherine did not answer, and Mrs Penniman went on. 'He is still very handsome, though of course he looks older now. I believe he married some lady somewhere in Europe. She died soon afterwards – as he said to me, she only passed through his life. The first thing he did was to ask me about you. He had heard you had never married; he seemed very much interested about that. He said you had been the real romance in his life.'

Catherine had listened silently, staring down at the ground. At last she spoke, 'Please do not say more.'

'But he very much wants to see you.'

'Please don't, Aunt Lavinia,' said Catherine, getting up

from her seat and moving quickly to the other window, where Mrs Penniman could not see that she was crying.

A week later they were again sitting in the front parlour. Catherine was working on some embroidery when Mrs Penniman suddenly said, 'Morris has sent you a message. He wishes to see you, Catherine. He is going away again, and wants to speak to you before he leaves. He says his happiness depends upon it.'

'My happiness does not,' said Catherine.

'He believes that you have never understood him, that you have never judged him rightly,' said Mrs Penniman. 'This is very painful for him, and he wants just a few minutes to explain. He wishes to meet you as a friend.'

Catherine listened without looking up from her embroidery. Then she said simply, 'Please say to Mr Townsend that I wish he would leave me alone.'

She had just finished speaking when the door bell rang. Catherine looked up at the clock; it was quarter past nine – a very late hour for visitors. She turned quickly to Mrs Penniman, who was blushing.

'Aunt Penniman,' she said, in a way that frightened her companion, 'what have you done?'

'My dearest Catherine,' said Mrs Penniman, avoiding her niece's eyes, 'just wait until you see him!'

Catherine had frightened her aunt, but she was also frightened herself and before she could prevent it, the servant had opened the door and announced his name.

'Mr Morris Townsend.'

'*Aunt Penniman, what have you done?*' Catherine said.

Catherine stood with her back turned to the door of the parlour. For some moments she remained still, feeling that he had come in. He had not spoken, however, and at last she turned round. She saw a gentleman standing in the middle of the room, from which her aunt had quietly left.

For a moment she did not recognize him. He was forty-five years old, fatter, with thinning hair and a thick beard.

'I have come because – I wanted to so much,' said Morris. It was the old voice, but it did not have the old charm.

'I think it was wrong of you to come,' said Catherine.

'Did Mrs Penniman not give you my message?'

'She told me something, but I did not understand.'

'I wish you would let *me* tell you.'

'I don't think it is necessary,' said Catherine.

'Not for you, perhaps, but for me.' He seemed to be coming nearer; Catherine turned away. 'Can we not be friends again?' he asked.

'We are not enemies,' said Catherine.

He moved close to her; she saw his beard, and the eyes above it, looking strange and hard. It was very different from his old – from his young – face. 'Catherine,' he murmured, 'I have never stopped thinking of you.'

'Please don't say these things,' she answered.

He looked at her again silently. 'It hurts you to see me here. I will go away; but you must allow me to come again.'

'Please don't come again,' she said. 'It is wrong of you. There is no reason for it. You behaved badly towards me.'

'That is not true,' cried Morris. 'You had your quiet life

with your father – I did not want to steal it from you.'

'Yes; I had that.'

Morris could not say that she also had some of her father's property; though he knew about Doctor Sloper's will. 'Catherine, have you never forgiven me?'

'I forgave you years ago, but we cannot be friends.'

'We can if we forget the past. We still have a future.'

'I can't forget – I don't forget,' said Catherine. 'You behaved too badly. I felt it very much; I felt it for years. I can't begin again – everything is dead and buried. I never expected to see you here again.'

Morris stood looking at her. 'Why have you never married?' he asked, suddenly.

'I didn't wish to marry.'

'Yes, you are rich, you are free. Marriage had nothing to offer you.' He looked around the room for a moment. 'Well, I had hoped that we could still be friends.'

'There is no possibility of that,' said Catherine.

'Goodbye, then,' said Morris.

He bowed, and she turned away. She stood there, looking at the ground, for some moments after she had heard him close the door of the room.

In the hall he found Mrs Penniman.

'Your plan did not work!' said Morris, putting on his hat.

'Is she so hard?' asked Mrs Penniman.

'She doesn't care a button for me,' said Morris. He stood for a moment, with his hat on. 'But why, then, has she never married?'

'Yes – why?' said Mrs Penniman. 'But you will not give up – you will come back?'

'Come back! Certainly not!' And Morris Townsend walked out of the house, leaving Mrs Penniman staring.

Catherine, meanwhile, in the parlour, picking up her embroidery, had seated herself with it again – for life.

Morris Townsend walked out of the house,
leaving Mrs Penniman staring.

GLOSSARY

admire   to like, and to have a very good opinion of someone

amazed   very surprised

announce   to make some information known to several people

blush *(v)*   to become red in the face because you are embarrassed, ashamed, shy, etc.

break off   to stop or end something suddenly

brilliant   extremely intelligent or clever

career   a job or a profession with good possibilities for the future

carriage   a vehicle for carrying people, pulled by horses

change your mind   to change your opinion or decision

charming   delightful; very pleasing

conceited   having much too good an opinion of yourself

consent   to give someone your agreement or permission

court *(v)*   to try to win a woman's love

despise   to have a very low opinion of someone (opposite of 'admire')

dizzy   feeling that everything is turning round and round and that you are going to fall

duty   something that you believe you must do

elegant   beautiful or well made; pleasing to look at

embarrassed   feeling uncomfortable or shy about something

embroidery   sewing pictures or patterns onto cloth with different coloured threads

engaged *(adj)*   having agreed to marry someone; *(n)* **engagement**

faithful   being true to someone; not changing towards them

fool   a person who behaves in a stupid way

forbid   to order someone not to do something

forgive   to say or show you are no longer angry with someone

give (someone) up to stop seeing or being friendly with someone
in general usually, mostly
in-law (e.g. **son-in-law**) a relative (e.g. son) by marriage only
insult *(v)* to speak in a very rude way that hurts somebody
means *(n)* money, etc.; what is needed to live comfortably
memory something remembered from the past
modest not thinking too well of yourself
murmur to speak in a very soft, low voice
navy a country's fighting ships and their crews
nod to bend your head forward quickly, to show agreement
parlour an old word for a sitting-room in a private house
part *(v)* to go away or separate from somebody; *(n)* **parting**
particular special; of more than usual importance
permission agreeing to allow someone to do something
position paid employment, a job
profession a job for which special training is necessary
property land or buildings which a person owns
reasonable thinking and behaving in a fair and sensible way
rent *(v)* to make regular payments for the use of a room or house
romance an exciting love affair (often not very serious or sensible)
romantic belonging to exciting love stories, not real life
sincere honest, with true feeling
sofa a long seat for two or three people
talent a natural ability to do something well
unjust not fair or right
upset unhappy, worried, miserable
widow a woman whose husband has died
will *(n)* a written statement about a person's money and
    property, saying who will inherit them after the person's death
wise sensible and experienced; showing good judgement

Washington Square

ACTIVITIES

Before Reading

1 **Read the back cover and the story introduction on the first page of the book. Match the adjectives with the people.**

Catherine Sloper   *Mrs Penniman*
Dr Austin Sloper   *Morris Townsend*

amusing, charming, clever, dull, foolish, gentle, handsome, interesting, quiet, rich, simple

2 **What is going to happen in the story? Can you guess? For each sentence, choose the best word(s) to complete it.**

1 Mrs Penniman *will / won't* be very friendly with Morris Townsend.
2 Catherine's father will say that Catherine *can / cannot* marry Morris Townsend.
3 Catherine will *agree / refuse* to marry Morris Townsend and later *refuse / agree*.
4 Catherine will *please / disappoint* her father in the end.
5 Dr Sloper will die and Catherine will inherit *all / some / none* of his money.
6 Catherine *will / won't* marry Morris Townsend and will be *happy / miserable*.

While Reading

Read Chapter 1, and then answer these questions.

1 Why was Dr Sloper successful?
2 Why was Dr Sloper lucky?
3 What happened to Dr Sloper's son?
4 What happened to Dr Sloper's wife?
5 Who came to live with Dr Sloper when Catherine was ten?
6 What did Dr Sloper want Catherine to become?
7 How did he feel about Catherine?
8 How did Catherine feel about her father?
9 Why was Catherine going to be rich?
10 Where did Dr Sloper move to in 1835?

Read Chapters 2 and 3. Are these sentences true (T) or false (F)? Rewrite the false ones with the correct information.

1 Morris Townsend was a cousin of Marian Almond.
2 Catherine talked a lot to Morris Townsend.
3 Mrs Penniman liked Morris Townsend.
4 Morris Townsend was working in an office.
5 Morris Townsend wanted to court Catherine.
6 Several young men had come courting Catherine before.
7 Morris Townsend had spent all his money amusing himself.
8 Dr Sloper didn't like Morris Townsend because he was poor.

Read Chapters 4 and 5. Who said this, and to whom? Who or what were they talking about?

1 'What is going on in this house?'
2 'But he has paid for it.'
3 'Perhaps I should give him another chance.'
4 'You advise me, then, not to give up hope?'
5 'I am their teacher.'
6 'We must do our duty; we must speak to my father.'
7 'You have gone very fast.'
8 'I accept that she will think I am cruel for a year.'
9 'I am very sorry for Catherine.'
10 'Don't let her marry him.'

Before you read Chapters 6 and 7, can you guess what will happen? Circle Y (Yes) or N (No) for each sentence.

1 Dr Sloper tells Catherine about Mrs Montgomery and she decides not to marry Morris. Y/N
2 Mrs Penniman helps Catherine to forget Morris. Y/N
3 Dr Sloper tells Catherine that she won't get his money if she marries Morris Townsend. Y/N
4 With her aunt's help, Catherine marries Morris secretly. Y/N
5 Catherine and Morris decide to wait before getting married. Y/N
6 Dr Sloper is amused by Catherine's situation. Y/N
7 Dr Sloper takes Catherine away to Europe. Y/N
8 Morris Townsend goes away to Europe. Y/N

Read Chapter 8. Choose the best question-word for these questions and then answer them.

What / Who / Why

1 . . . thought that Morris would make Catherine a bad husband?

2 . . . did Catherine expect from her father?

3 . . . did Catherine make Morris promise?

4 . . . did Morris decide to give Catherine up?

5 . . . wanted Catherine and Morris to have a last parting?

6 . . . did Catherine think that Morris would not come back?

7 . . . reason did Morris give in his letter for leaving Catherine?

8 . . . did Catherine feel when she got Morris's letter?

9 . . . did Catherine tell her father about her engagement?

Before you read Chapter 9 (*Morris returns*), can you guess what happens? Circle Y (Yes) or N (No) for each of these sentences.

1 Everyone finds out the truth about Catherine's broken engagement. Y/N

2 Several other men ask Catherine to marry them. Y/N

3 Catherine promises her father that she will never marry Morris Townsend. Y/N

4 Dr Sloper changes his will before he dies, and does not leave Catherine all his money. Y/N

5 After Dr Sloper's death, Morris Townsend comes back and Catherines marries him. Y/N

After Reading

1 **Whose thoughts are these? Who are they thinking about and when? Then find words in the story which mean the opposite of the words in italic.**

1 'I don't want to marry her if her father disinherits her. She's very *dull*, and I must have money – I'm tired of being *poor*. But that last meeting was so *difficult* and *unpleasant*. I won't go back again – I'll write her a letter instead . . .'

2 'It was very *foolish* of Lavinia to be so *friendly* with him – and now look what's happened. He's gone away and the poor girl is so *miserable*. I must be *kind* to her.'

3 'He's so *handsome* and *self-confident*. I don't know why my cousin said he was *conceited* – I thought he was very *sincere* and natural. I *admired* him very much. My aunt *liked* him too, and she thought that he was very *clever* . . .'

4 'I never thought that she would *amuse* me so much. But she's too *soft* and *weak* to fight her own battles, and he's not a suitable husband for her. He's *selfish* and *lazy* – and his sister has just told me that I am *right*.'

5 'He seemed *annoyed* with me today. I know I advised a secret marriage last week, but that was before Austin spoke to me so *coldly*. Young people are never *grateful* . . .'

2 Complete the conversation that Mrs Penniman had with Morris Townsend at Marian Almond's party. Use as many words as you like.

MRS PENNIMAN: So you are a cousin of Arthur Townsend. Why haven't we seen you here in New York before?

MORRIS: _____.

MRS PENNIMAN: How interesting! I have never travelled much myself. And why have you returned to New York?

MORRIS: _____.

MRS PENNIMAN: So are you living with your parents?

MORRIS: _____.

MRS PENNIMAN: I'm sure that makes your sister very happy. I expect you help her with the children?

MORRIS: _____.

MRS PENNIMAN: Oh, like me! I have lived with Catherine since she was ten years old, and have been a teacher to her.

MORRIS: _____?

MRS PENNIMAN: Yes, she died when Catherine was a baby. But I have tried to be a mother to her. She's looking very fine tonight, don't you think?

MORRIS: _____.

MRS PENNIMAN: Yes, it *is* a beautiful dress – very expensive, of course.

MORRIS: _____?

MRS PENNIMAN: Oh no, money's not a problem. Catherine will inherit a large fortune from her father, you know.

3 **Complete the letter that Morris wrote to Catherine after he went to Philadelphia. Choose the best word for each gap.**

Dear Catherine

I am _____ to you from Philadelphia. _____ am afraid that I _____ going to be away _____ a long time on _____ business. I will never _____ you, but I couldn't _____ myself if you lost _____ your money because of _____. It is better for _____ to separate than to _____ each other unhappy. Please _____ that I am only _____ of you. My dearest _____ is for you to _____ a happy and peaceful _____. This will not be _____ if we marry. You _____ your father and want _____ please him, but he _____ be very angry and _____ his will if you _____ not obey him. You _____ marry a man that _____ father likes, or give _____ your property and be _____. So I have gone _____, because I do not _____ to injure you. I _____ when I come back, _____ will be able to _____ as friends.

Morris

4 **Imagine that the story had a different ending. Choose one of these possibilities and use the notes to write about what happened. Finish the story with your own ideas.**

1 Catherine not go to Europe / marry Morris secretly / Dr Sloper never forgive her / no money / . . .

2 Catherine come back from Europe / marry Morris / Dr Sloper forgive her / Catherine inherit fortune / . . .

5 **Do you agree (A) or disagree (D) with these statements? Explain why.**

  1 Dr Sloper: 'You are good for nothing unless you are clever.'

  2 Mrs Penniman: 'My dear Austin, you are making a great mistake if you think that Catherine is a weak woman.'

  3 Mrs Almond (about Morris Townsend): 'He will make Catherine a bad husband.'

  4 Catherine (about her father): 'And I think he despises me . . . Of course it isn't my fault, but neither is it his fault.'

  5 Morris Townsend (to Catherine): 'Yes, you are rich, you are free. Marriage had nothing to offer you.'

6 **Do you think that *Washington Square* is a good title for this story? Would you prefer one of these titles instead? Why?**

  Rich Man's Daughter   A Cruel Father   Catherine
  Waiting for Morris   A Foolish Girl   A Dollar Romance

7 **Which of these qualities are important when you decide to marry someone? Put them in order (1 for the most important). Explain why. Add any other ideas of your own.**

  It is important to marry someone . . .
  • who has a lot of money.
  • that your parents choose for you.
  • with the same interests as you.
  • that your parents like.
  • who is handsome/pretty.
  • that you love.
  • who loves you.
  • who is clever.
  • who is good. ·
  • that you like.

ABOUT THE AUTHOR

Henry James was born in 1843 in New York. His father was a writer and his brother William was a well-known philosopher. Henry went to schools in New York and Europe, and then studied law at Harvard. In 1865 he began to write for magazines, and in 1875, his first important novel, *Roderick Hudson*, appeared. He moved to Europe in that same year, living first in Paris, and then for more than twenty years in London.

Washington Square appeared in 1881, and describes New York as it was when James was young. He did not like the story himself, perhaps because he wrote it fast and felt it was too short. But it has been compared to the novels of Jane Austen for the clear and exact way that he shows us the characters and their life.

His next novels, including *The Portrait of a Lady* (1881), describe the effect of the 'old' society of Europe meeting the new world of the United States. He then wrote a number of books which looked in more detail at English people. His last three great novels (*The Wings of a Dove, The Ambassadors* and *The Golden Bowl*), which were written after he moved to Sussex in 1898, returned to the idea of differences between Americans and Europeans. As well as novels, Henry James wrote short stories, including the famous ghost story, *The Turn of the Screw* (1898), travel books and plays – although these were not very successful. Several of his novels have been made into films in recent years.

Henry James became a British subject in 1915, a year before his death in 1916.

ABOUT BOOKWORMS

OXFORD BOOKWORMS LIBRARY

Classics • True Stories • Fantasy & Horror • Human Interest
Crime & Mystery • Thriller & Adventure

The OXFORD BOOKWORMS LIBRARY offers a wide range of original and adapted stories, both classic and modern, which take learners from elementary to advanced level through six carefully graded language stages:

Stage 1 (400 headwords)	**Stage 4** (1400 headwords)
Stage 2 (700 headwords)	**Stage 5** (1800 headwords)
Stage 3 (1000 headwords)	**Stage 6** (2500 headwords)

More than fifty titles are also available on cassette, and there are many titles at Stages 1 to 4 which are specially recommended for younger learners. In addition to the introductions and activities in each Bookworm, resource material includes photocopiable test worksheets and Teacher's Handbooks, which contain advice on running a class library and using cassettes, and the answers for the activities in the books.

Several other series are linked to the OXFORD BOOKWORMS LIBRARY. They range from highly illustrated readers for young learners, to playscripts, non-fiction readers, and unsimplified texts for advanced learners.

Oxford Bookworms Starters	*Oxford Bookworms Factfiles*
Oxford Bookworms Playscripts	*Oxford Bookworms Collection*

Details of these series and a full list of all titles in the OXFORD BOOKWORMS LIBRARY can be found in the *Oxford English* catalogues. A selection of titles from the OXFORD BOOKWORMS LIBRARY can be found on the next pages.

Cranford

ELIZABETH GASKELL

Retold by Kate Mattock

Life in the small English town of Cranford seems very quiet and peaceful. The ladies of Cranford lead tidy, regular lives. They make their visits between the hours of twelve and three, give little evening parties, and worry about their maid-servants. But life is not always smooth – there are little arguments and jealousies, sudden deaths and unexpected marriages . . .

Mrs Gaskell's timeless picture of small-town life in the first half of the nineteenth century has delighted readers for nearly 150 years.

Silas Marner

GEORGE ELIOT

Retold by Clare West

In a hole under the floorboards Silas Marner the linen-weaver keeps his gold. Every day he works hard at his weaving, and every night he takes the gold out and holds the bright coins lovingly, feeling them and counting them again and again. The villagers are afraid of him and he has no family, no friends. Only the gold is his friend, his delight, his reason for living.

But what if a thief should come in the night and take his gold away? What will Silas do then? What could possibly comfort him for the loss of his only friend?

Little Women

LOUISA MAY ALCOTT

Retold by John Escott

When Christmas comes for the four March girls, there is no money for expensive presents and they give away their Christmas breakfast to a poor family. But there are no happier girls in America than Meg, Jo, Beth, and Amy. They miss their father, of course, who is away at the Civil War, but they try hard to be good so that he will be proud of his 'little women' when he comes home.

This heart=warming story of family life has been popular for more than a hundred years.

A Tale of Two Cities

CHARLES DICKENS

Retold by Ralph Mowat

'The Marquis lay there, like stone, with a knife pushed into his heart. On his chest lay a piece of paper, with the words: *Drive him fast to his grave. This is from JACQUES.*'

The French Revolution brings terror and death to many people. But even in these troubled times people can still love and be kind. They can be generous and true-hearted . . . and brave.

Three Men in a Boat

JEROME K. JEROME

Retold by Diane Mowat

'I like work. I find it interesting . . . I can sit and look at it for hours.'

With ideas like this, perhaps it is not a good idea to spend a holiday taking a boat trip up the River Thames. But this is what the three friends decide to do. It is the sort of holiday that is fun to remember afterwards, but not so much fun to wake up to early on a cold, wet morning.

This famous book has made people laugh all over the world for a hundred years . . . and they are still laughing.

The Bride Price

BUCHI EMECHETA

Retold by Rosemary Border

When her father dies, Aku-nna and her young brother have no one to look after them. They are welcomed by their uncle because of Aku-nna's 'bride price' – the money that her future husband will pay for her.

In her new, strange home one man is kind to her and teaches her to become a woman. Soon they are in love, although everyone says he is not a suitable husband for her. The more the world tries to separate them, the more they are drawn together – until, finally, something has to break.